WHEN A CHILD DIES

by Daniel T. Hans

Desert Ministries, Inc.
Palm Beach, Florida

Dedicated to Laura Grace,
a beautiful gift,
briefly in my arms,
always in my heart.

Note to the Reader

Immediately after the loss of a child, numbed shock prevails. Merely trying to survive the emotional trauma of each day is all that grieving parents can do. Any attempt to reflect upon faith and hope during this time is simply too difficult.

For these reasons, this book should not be given to grieving parents immediately after their loss. Weeks or months later, however, as the transition toward moving on with life begins, they may find this book helpful. Until that time, what can you do? Read this book yourself, reflect upon your own faith, and do as Job's three friends did — sit with your grieving loved ones in silence. Your presence will remind them that God is with them in times of sorrow.

Editor's Introduction

In your hands is a precious book. It will touch your heart and hopes. While it is primarily for those who have walked the lonely road of losing a child, it will benefit each and all who read it. Dr. Hans and his wife have traveled that road. Their daughter died just after her third birthday. The integrity of his search to recover his faith and equilibrium is shared openly and honestly.

Desert Ministries is pleased to offer you this book in our continuing journey to bring the living waters of Christ into the bleak deserts of our lives. We are proud to have Dr. Hans among our group of authors.

At the end of the book you will find a list of other publications which we will make available on your request. Meanwhile, may God bless you and keep you in His care.

Rev. Richard M. Cromie, Ph.D., D.D.
President, Desert Ministries, Inc.

WHEN A CHILD DIES

Table of Contents

Introduction

This book is meant for people of faith who have lost a loved one — particularly a child — and for the people who love them. No book can adequately address everyone's response to such overwhelming loss. Nor can any book fully capture all the dynamics of faith as it is questioned and reformed following such a tragedy. Our grief and convictions vary greatly…. yet certain feelings and responses are common to all of us.

In this book I share my personal struggle to find light in the darkness that encompassed me and shelter in the storm that raged about me during the illness and death of my little girl. It is my hope that through my experience you will better understand your own struggles in relation to your faith in God.

Perhaps there is a Laura Grace somewhere in your life. As you weather your ordeal, you will come to know firsthand the full range of emotions that accompany faith's attempt to wrest some shred of meaning from the pain. The good news is that the encompassing darkness breaks when rays of hope shine through. The storm's fury weakens and passes with time. Finally, God gives us the strength to move forward, ready for whatever lies ahead and confident in the One who goes with us.

Everyone Loses Someone

To lose a parent is to lose the past; to lose a spouse or close friend is to lose the present; to lose a child is to lose the future. While the loss of a loved one is never easy, memories of the parent, spouse or friend help fill the aching void. But when a child dies, our dreams are snatched away, leaving an empty yearning for what could have been. I know this yearning in the depth of my soul, for my cradle of hope was robbed of its dream. I have faced every parent's worst nightmare and now stare into the haunting eyes of what never will be.

For the first thirty-three years of my life, I was spared the agonizing pain of loss that befalls so many people when they become victims of personal tragedy. Although I knew firsthand the agony of a disappointing loss in sports, a broken heart in romance and a guilty conscience in sin, these were skinned knees compared to the loss of my dream.

In my work as a pastor, I often assist people in walking through the valley of the shadow of death. When I preach at funeral services, I discuss how death is the constant shadow of life. Like our own shadow, it follows us persistently. But when death closes the gap and strikes its victim, it catches those who are close to that person off guard. The shock is as startling as if our own shadow had reached out and slapped us across the face.

In the Advent season of 1985, I was preparing my congregation for the celebration of Christ's birth when the shadow of death raised its hand over me and began its back swing. It did not strike this time, but soon would.

As Christmas in our Connecticut home approached, my wife, Beth, and I were filled with anticipation and apprehension. We were in our seventh month of pregnancy with our second child, and we excitedly awaited the February due date. However, we also anxiously awaited the results of a series of medical tests on our firstborn child, Laura.

Laura always seemed to be connected to testing. Over the three years that Beth and I had tried to become pregnant, we had pursued many types of medical tests. When Laura was born, we were ecstatic. We named her Laura Grace - Laura, because the name was beautiful like her, and Grace, because we saw her as a gift from God. If Laura was a gift from God, then how could her life be taken from us? Was God an Indian giver?

Laura was two-and-a-half years old that Christmas as we awaited her test results. For several months we had taken her to various doctors seeking an answer to her walking and balance problems. The initial diagnosis of mild cerebral palsy due to umbilical cord strangulation at birth proved erroneous as her condition worsened. One neurologist ordered a CT scan of the brain and questioned us about our family backgrounds. I sensed he was concerned about a possible genetic problem that might also affect the child Beth was carrying. His questions heightened our already soaring fears.

I will never forget the phone call I received from that doctor. He said, "Reverend Hans, I want you to listen very carefully. The child your wife is carrying will be a healthy baby." I replied, "Thank you, but what about Laura?" His silence was foreboding. He then told me that the CT scan revealed a tumor the size of an orange at the base of her brain. The impact was like a hand grenade exploding in my chest. He used the term "medulloblastoma" which, if I had known then what I know now, would have felt like two hand grenades. Medulloblastoma is a very aggressive cancer with a bleak survival rate. The doctor recommended immediate brain surgery.

As we transported Laura to nearby Yale-New Haven Hospital, I remember a double terror gripping me. I feared prematurely losing one child while prematurely gaining another. As concerned as I was for my daughter, I was equally concerned for her pregnant mother. Laura was admitted to the hospital that evening with surgery scheduled for early the next morning. The date was Friday, December 13th.

That night sleep escaped me. In the early morning hours of darkness, I began to think about Laura and death, family and love, God and hope. My thoughts took the form of a letter I composed to Laura. It read:

Dear Laura,
You are sleeping now, although not here with us. Your Mommy and I are awake and missing you terribly. As I look back on yesterday and the discovery of the tumor, I can only describe it as the worst day of my life I think it's the worst that could happen, and yet it isn't.

When the doctor told me that they found a tumor inside that smart little head of yours, my worst fears took the witness stand. Soon they will shave off those Goldilocks curls of yours. Do you remember how you describe Goldilocks' hair in the story? You say, "She has beautiful blond hair just like me." Well, not anymore, princess.

When they start cutting your hair, you will begin a journey. You will not discover anything, because you will be

3

sleeping. The doctors will be the explorers. They will travel below your golden locks to try to make you better.

Mommy and I know that the coming days and weeks will be difficult for you and for us. We are haunted by "the worst that could happen." Fear causes this, and fear has such power. We fear losing you. It's the worst that could happen to us... and yet it isn't.

For all the fear that drives our hearts and minds to work overtime, we can also feel a calm. It is the calm with which we put you to bed at night as we remind you that Mommy and Daddy love you and God loves you, too. We are putting ourselves to bed with the reminder that, no matter what happens, God loves all of us.

As you sleep now in the hospital away from us, we fear the worst. Yet we are awakened to the comfort that God's great love conquers our worst fears. Goodnight, Laura.

Love always,
Daddy

The neurosurgeon told us in no uncertain terms that Laura might not survive the surgery, due to the extent and location of the tumor. He also told us that if she survived, she would not be the same child. Certain physical and mental capacities would certainly be lost to the scalpel. She did survive the operation. However, she lost many of her verbal skills as well as the ability to pull the red wagon she requested that Christmas. She also lost the entire back of her skull when it was removed during surgery, then covered over only with scalp. This was the surgeon's way of leaving the door open for a return visit. He was right; we did not get back the same child we delivered to surgery. But she was alive along with our hope.

After a four-week hospital stay, Laura came home, bald and battered, for a belated Christmas celebration and a new red wagon. I returned to my pastoral duties from a leave of absence. My first Sunday back in the pulpit, I spoke about hope. To the church family that had supported us with their prayers, loving notes and phone calls, I tried to offer something solid to grasp in a sea of uncertainty.

Drawing upon a verse from the Old Testament in which God promises, "I will make the Valley of Achor a door of hope" (Hosea 2:15), I began my message with this thought: Most of us have been there already, although we did not plan to take the trip. Some of us have yet to wander into its disturbing terrain. All of us will journey there sometime in our life. It is an uninviting place, terrifying, depressing, ominous. The Valley of Achor, loosely translated, means the valley of trouble.

My congregation was familiar with the Valley of Achor. Like any group of humans, they had their litany of troubles: deaths, divorces, loss of innocence, losses of friendship, losses of abilities. All of us suffer some type of loss at some time in our life. Therefore, we all need assistance navigating the journey in which loss and grief are inevitable. However, one loss sinks below most other tragedies in the valley of pain and confusion: there is something so unnatural, so untimely and so unsettling about losing a child that it shakes our very foundation. The magnitude of pain and fear surrounding my daughter's illness made our valley of trouble a canyon with walls so steep and high that darkness covered the quaking floor, where we groped for direction and meaning.

In that dark valley, hope became my resource. It began to take on new meaning as never before. Until Laura's diagnosis, I had felt in control of my life and future. However, as I anguished through her six-hour surgery aware she might not survive, I realized that her life and our future were completely outside my control. Parents feel threatened beyond words when control over the well-being and safety of their children is denied them. There was not a damn thing I could do to help Laura. All I could do was hope there was a purpose to this and a presence, unseen at the moment, yet greater than the moment.

Everyone Struggles with Faith Amid Loss

Laura was home, but far from home free. The valley was still deep and dark. Her tumor was malignant, and the most effective procedure for destroying the residue left after surgery was radiation. At her young age, however, heavy doses of radiation to her brain and spinal cord would produce permanent mental and physical impairment. Therefore, her doctors recommended starting her on chemotherapy. Hopefully, this would delay the need for radiation six to nine months while Laura completed a vital growth stage.

We were told that the drugs Laura would receive every day for two weeks would be relatively mild. Nevertheless, her treatments caused violent vomiting, severe weight loss and total hair loss. During the two weeks following treatment, she was extremely susceptible to infection. Her life alternated between protective isolation at home and trips to the cancer clinic. Her parents' life became one of watching her battle and wondering about this difficult journey called life.

During this period, when I was consumed with Laura's illness and the uncertainty of her future, I puzzled over the "what-abouts" of life. Had I stopped to reflect on having been spared the agony of personal tragedy for so many years, I would have concluded that my good fortune was due to

God's blessing on those who faithfully seek to serve the Lord. However, like Job, who lost everything that meant something to him through no fault of his own and for no apparent reason, I began to question my faith. When life is easy and the path is paved with blessings, our faith escapes these questions. However, when starvation kills thousands, a downed jet claims hundreds, a random act of violence destroys a family or a child – my child – is diagnosed with brain cancer, how can we not rattle the gates of heaven demanding to know, "O God, what is this all about?" There isn't a person of faith who hasn't asked the Almighty, "Why?"

Throughout Laura's illness, death and the long years since, I have struggled to hold on to the two loves that give my life definition, two loves which are assaulted when personal tragedy strikes. The first is my love for God. The second is my love of life, with all its idiosyncrasies and inconsistencies. Regardless of the severity of our loss and anguish, we must find a way to affirm and embrace our conviction that life is a good and wonderful gift. Our pain must never be allowed to negate the grace inherent in life.

My daughter's illness was not a result of sin or moral failing, either hers or ours. It was an evil, but not a moral evil. It was a natural evil — a confusing inconsistency which is grossly unfair. Tragic as it may be, there seems to be an element of fairness in the death of a reckless driver. But the death of an innocent passenger is unfair. Even more unfair is the death of a child to cancer. However, in the midst of the unfairness and randomness that characterize many of life's events, goodness and grace persist. Embracing these qualities enables us to endure the terror of the moment.

Those who lose sight and let go of life's goodness and grace find that darkness descends without promise of a new dawn. When this happens, we either withdraw or become cynical, refusing to hope again or to love again for fear of losing again. I recall meeting a mother in a support group for parents who had lost children to cancer. Her teenage son had died of leukemia ten years earlier and she still grieved as if his death had been yesterday. She had transformed his room into a shrine, changing nothing from the moment he died. She built a wall around her heart, pushing away her husband and other son. In essence, the day her son died she died, too. She did not see the difference between walking through the valley of the shadow of death and getting stuck there.

While I think it tragic that this pained and confused mother stopped loving and living, I understand her need to withdraw into a protective shell. It is very hard to keep going when our joy in life has been taken away. I wholeheartedly agree with a saying I once heard, "Life is good, but living is hard."

In the face of hardship, some of us give up on life. Others give up on faith. I have struggled to hold on to God. We let go of God when we leave our anger unexpressed or worse, when we deny our pain through a superficial "praise God for everything" kind of faith. I have never been able to praise God for my daughter's cancer, nor will I ever praise Him for my loss. Life and faith are too important to me to take them so lightly.

During my long ordeal, I repeatedly wondered if my sorrow-scarred faith would survive my loss and if so, what new expression would it take. Through my experience ministering to suffering people and now as a fellow sufferer, I discovered common misconceptions about the relationship between personal tragedy and personal faith. In the course of this book, I will address three misconceptions that can do

9

serious damage to our love for life and love for God.

One misconception is the belief that the Bible answers the question, "Why?" We are sure that somewhere God provides an answer to this tragic question that haunts our faith. In this age of information, we are convinced that there is an answer to every question, a cause for every effect, a resolution for every dilemma. When we cannot find a convincing explanation for our tragedy, our faith is thrown into a tailspin.

Trying to reconcile faith with loss drives many thinking believers into a maze of dead-end philosophical tunnels, and many feeling believers to abandon church or synagogue and give up on prayer. How does one make peace with the love, power and goodness of God in the presence of pain, suffering and evil? Attempts to resolve this tension are as old as humankind.

Ancient Greek philosophers explained it through the concept of dualism. Dualism holds that the universe has two coexisting, equal powers, or gods. One is good; the other is evil. They are in constant combat, with neither achieving ultimate victory. Greek mythology plays out this good-god-versus-bad-god theme. Christianity falls into this game of dualism when it gives too much credit and power to Satan, claiming that tragedies are the work of the devil. While as the saying goes, "Give the devil its due," I caution against giving the devil more than its due. God alone is sovereign. God alone has ultimate power and victory. No realm of life is isolated from His goodness. But if this is true, then that which we call evil must be linked somehow to the will of God. From the moment of Laura's diagnosis, I began a long struggle to grasp how God might be present in my little girl's suffering. This struggle was the attempt of a hurting man to find rays of hope.

Demotion is a different approach to the tension between faith and loss. Here God is demoted from a position of supreme power in order to allow for the existence of evil. God is loving but limited, mighty but not almighty. This view presents a finite God who desires to do more in the face of suffering, but is unable. I am left uneasy anytime God is demoted to One-who-is-less-than-all-powerful. We need God to be more than just another big-hearted, well-meaning-but-inept friend. We need a source of strength beyond all other strengths. We need God to be Almighty.

A third attempt to reconcile divine love and power with human tragedy is denial. Some faith groups take this route. They deny the seriousness of illness and evil, claiming them to be illusions that can be conquered by a "mind over matter" or "name it and claim it" approach. Try telling a parent who has watched a daughter lose her mental and physical abilities to a brain tumor that cancer is just an illusion! Try explaining to a wife who stands beside her husband's fresh grave that death is not real! In the midst of Laura's chemotherapy, I received a phone call from a man I did not know who had obtained my name from a mutual acquaintance. This Christian had heard about my little girl's cancer and offered his healing services to us. He claimed he had developed a successful technique of healing. His attitude toward Laura's cancer was that it was no problem; God can handle it. When I declined his offer, he could not understand my "lack of faith." More to the point, he seemed not to understand the seriousness of Laura's cancer. True faith never denies the seriousness of human problems and does not reduce the mystery of God to a gimmick or technique.

A fourth approach is that of despair. Our faith in God can be compared to a computer system, where our understanding of God's ways is the software that makes our faith run. Some of us have software which declares that God protects us from all evil. On our screen of faith is the icon of a smiling face that, when clicked, reads, "Bad things don't happen to good people." When we find ourselves confronted with the suffering of an innocent loved one, our software cannot process the tragedy. Our faith computer cannot spit out the answer to, "Why?" In despair, we pull the plug and stop believing in God. When a person's faith allows no room for unanswered questions, the faith becomes very vulnerable.

Tragedy drives some of us to blame ourselves — damn ourselves — for what happened. For those of us who lose a child, self-damnation is common, whether we could have done something to help our child or not. It is natural for parents to blame themselves. After all, is our job not to protect our kids? Standing beside a child's grave makes us feel like we have failed our parental duty. With Laura's diagnosis of cancer, self-damnation made its ugly appearance in Beth's and my thoughts. We wondered, is God punishing us? What did we do to cause this tumor? How could we have prevented it? Even now, parental guilt still rings our doorbell. It persists because we are accustomed to thinking that every problem has a solution, every effect a cause, every question an answer. Something more than an answer is needed. Yet an answer to, "Why?" would not have made any difference. It would not have restored my daughter. I needed — and still need — something greater than an answer.

In this world, created and sustained by an all-loving, all-powerful, all-good God, my little girl had a horrible disease. There was no cause for it and no explanation. It was not a judgment. It just happened. In the face of this dilemma, I found strength in two convictions.

The first is that life goes on. Tragedy takes innocent victims, and those who are close grieve over the unfairness of it all. Yet, life goes on. During Laura's chemotherapy, I shared a tragedy with the entire nation when the space shuttle Challenger exploded, killing all seven astronauts on board. A few days later, a camera crew interviewed the residents of Concord, New Hampshire, the home of teacher/astronaut Christa McAuliffe, who perished on the spacecraft. An old timer, when asked how the loss would affect the residents of Concord, answered, "We will grieve our loss, but life will go on."

The second conviction stands on the promise that whatever happens, God is with us. This conviction was made clear to me in a powerful newspaper illustration printed a few days after the Challenger disaster, when I was beginning to wonder how long Laura would be with us. It pictured the Challenger racing toward the stars. There, in the black night, was a dim image of a great outstretched hand receiving the Challenger gently into its palm. I knew this hand would be there for Laura, if she did not survive her cancer.

Sometimes Our Faith Begins to Change

When faced with the nagging "what-abouts" of life and the haunting "whys" of faith, what I wanted most was not what I needed most: I sought an answer to why my little girl had cancer. I needed a presence in my pain and confusion. I needed a story of faith and hope. Then I began to place the story of how God's Son suffered alongside the story of my daughter's suffering. While the connection did not answer my question, it did remind me that God understood. My faith held firm, but began to change.

Laura made a slow but steady recovery from her surgery. During those three post-operative months things looked brighter. Our second child was born. Laura, who had been saying throughout Beth's pregnancy, "We don't want no boys," got her wish. She beamed with delight as she sat on the couch, clumsily holding her baby sister, Amy. Since Laura's overall condition was improving, we put her to work caring for Amy. Her task was teaching her sister to smile, and she did a masterful job: the fruit of her labor lives on undeniably in her sister's grin.

Easter, that most glorious day of the year, saw our entire family together in church for the first time since before Christmas. Beth wore a colorful Easter hat, Amy donned a baby bonnet, I wore my preacher's countenance and Laura displayed her new wig. The day's joy was short-lived, however, when Laura began experiencing severe muscle cramps that seized her entire body. Neither codeine nor morphine brought relief. She was readmitted to the hospital for the fourth time in as many months. The days and weeks that had been progressing with such pleasure were jolted to a cruel halt as our future once again was put on hold.

Waiting is never easy, regardless of one's mental attitude or faith. I spent the first week of Laura's fourth hospital stay beside her bed. I waited as doctors tried to find the cause of the cramps that seized her body every twenty minutes. Then I waited as they sought a reason for her violent vomiting of blood and bile. I waited beside her bed in the Intensive Care Unit as the medical team puzzled over the seizures that jerked her unconscious body. Each day I waited for her condition to improve.

During this hospital episode, I was cruelly reminded that I was not in control. This goes against my temperament. My nature is to be a manager, an administrator, to "sweat the little things" and to ensure that all goes according to plan — my plan. Laura's condition took away my control. Her illness taught me how truly helpless I am, and how I must learn to wait for the Lord. "Those who wait for the Lord shall renew their strength" (Isaiah 40: 31 NRSV).

The invitation to "wait for the Lord" is not an admonition to sit on our hands and view ourselves as passive pawns on the board of the divine chess master. Those who wait for the Lord shall be renewed so they may rise to the occasion and move forward, even when the course is uphill and pitted with obstacles and control is beyond their grasp. Waiting for God is not losing heart. It is finding a new heart that embraces the life-giving grace of the One whom death could not defeat. Waiting for God is not hibernating in hopelessness. It is germinating into a stronger person who finds hope to face the future by trusting the future to God. As the old gospel hymn resounds, "I do not know what the future holds, but I know Who holds the future." To wait for God's help is to continue working, praying and hoping, even in the face of change without improvement.

For seven days straight I waited. Finally, an answer came. It was one of those moments that, when it finally arrives, you wish you were still waiting. A CT scan of the brain confirmed our fears: the chemotherapy had been ineffective. The tumor was growing. More tumor could be removed through surgery, and Laura's chances of surviving this round were far better than the first round. However, the degree of permanent mental and physical impairment she would suffer would be uncertain. We were confident our beloved Laura would emerge from the operating room, but we were not confident what her functional ability would be.

Aware of the crisis confronting us, we mobilized a network of prayer in churches throughout the United States. Seldom is one person the subject of so much petitioning as was Laura. Many of these prayers sought Laura's healing. To the hopeful optimism I added my own note of sober realism. Hope had been my companion throughout this ordeal, but my hope was not blind to the deadly consequences of cancer.

My realism led me to reflect upon the greatness of God. I pondered whether or not my view of God and my prayers to God were too big, too exaggerated. I had read somewhere that what we ask from God reveals what we assume about God. This reveals the cause behind much of the frustration and disappointment that invade our faith when God falls short of our expectations. If we looked closely, we would find that much of our pondering, praying, and questioning is misdirected due to our false assumptions about God. Our faith is grounded in the greatness of God. We are right in calling Him eternal, almighty, supreme and all-knowing. What we must keep in mind is that these descriptions of God's greatness exist within the bounds that He has set by the way He has acted throughout history. Problems arise for us when our view of God exceeds God's own actions and intentions.

Every week starting with Laura's initial diagnosis, Beth and I received cards and letters of support and encouragement from friends, acquaintances and strangers. In some of those notes, people shared stories of parents who had prayed for their children's health and the diseases were healed. The implication was that if Beth and I prayed enough Laura would be healed. This is false logic. Just because something occurs in the life of a person of faith does not mean it will occur in the lives of others with the same faith. In the Bible, God delivers some people from their struggles, and we hear their praises for God's protection. However, the pages of the Bible and of church history are filled with the bloodstains of others who were not delivered from their struggles.

Our view of God is too big if we make an individual situation the standard for all similar situations. To seek a God who solves all problems and brings success to all who come to Him is to seek a God who exists only in our wishes. One of the most helpful things in my own search for God was spoken by a man whose God was not too big for me to find. He said that God does not take us out of our problems, but steps into our problems to be with us. That made sense to me and helped me see how I can live for God in this life with all its struggles, hardships and disappointments.

In the months after those dreaded words "tumor" and

"cancer" forced their way into my mental vocabulary, I longed to see my little girl regain use of her legs and coordination of her arms. I dreamed of hearing the doctors say, "We have no medical explanation for it, but Laura's cancer has disappeared." I did not see nor hear either. No miracle occurred. I guess I could have demanded that God show His power in some miraculous way, but this would have prevented me from seeing the evidence of God's marvelous work already at hand. Instead of looking for signs of God in miracles, I learned to see His work in medical science. Rather than seeking to witness God's touch solely through a recovery of Laura's abilities, I began to see His touch in the gentle care offered by her nurses and therapists. This freed my faith to see God at work in ways other than those I expected or demanded. I realized that if I could not see God in the care being given to Laura — regardless of the outcome — then my God was too big.

While Laura was going through a time of change marked by a deterioration in health, I, by the sheer grace of God, was also going through a time of change marked by a transformation of faith. I was beginning to view God less in terms of power and more in terms of presence, less in terms of miracles and more in terms of mercy, less in terms of grandeur and more in terms of grace. This change did not detract from God's power and grandeur; it simply helped me feel God's closeness. I would need this retooled faith to face my future.

In retrospect, one of the discoveries I made is that God often prepares us for the next leg of the journey without making us aware of it. Two experiences of mystery and grace that crossed my path months before Laura's ordeal began helped prepare me for her struggle and mine. About one year before her diagnosis, at a spiritual retreat I was leading, I awoke from a dream with a strange mixture of panic and peace. The feeling of panic arose from the premonition that someone in my family had cancer. I did not know who, but suspected it was me. Tethered to the panic was an equally powerful sense of peace. Something told me that everything would be okay. That dream prompted me to consider what I would do if someone in my family did have cancer. There was preparatory grace in that dream.

The second experience was more profound and formative. Nine months before Laura's diagnosis, I was asked by a local funeral home director to conduct a funeral for friends whose two-year-old daughter had died of leukemia. Wanting to meet the parents personally and learn about their child, I visited their home. In her photos, this little blond two-year-old looked remarkably like my daughter. She had slept in a crib, just like my little girl did, and had some of the same toys. I left that home realizing that in order to offer a public farewell for their little girl, I would have to come to terms with what it would be like to say farewell to my own. Within nine months of that child's funeral, my little girl was on the same cancer floor of the same hospital.

In these two mysterious experiences of grace and with my own maturing expectations of God, I believe I was being prepared for what lay ahead.

Sometimes We Get Angry with God

The much-feared side effects of Laura's second round of surgery came to pass. Although she survived the operation, she was seriously impaired. Her entire right side, formerly smooth and fluid in motion, was now spastic to the point of being useless. Her strength vanished. Her ability to sit unassisted disappeared. As if all this were not enough, her smile, which had been a beacon of joy to us, lost its radiance. Never again would she enjoy riding on her swing, or "whee" as she called it, coloring with crayons or holding her baby sister. One additional forfeiture carried with it good news: on the surgeon's table lay more of her tumor. Somehow removing the bulk of this foreign invader made the other deprivations more tolerable, but only for a brief time.

After a two-week hospital stay, Laura returned home, only to be readmitted two weeks later. The muscle cramping had returned, suggesting additional tumor growth. Since chemotherapy had been unsuccessful and further surgery would be too damaging, radiation therapy was the only choice. Once again our hope was put to a harsh test. For seven weeks, five times a week, Laura received radiation. Throughout these early summer weeks, we continued to pursue physical therapy each day at home in the hope she would regain some strength and basic skills. However, her physical condition and mental acuity continued to weaken. Initially, we attributed the decline to the side effects of radiation and

21

hoped it would be temporary, but this was not the case.

The home care took its toll on Beth and me. Shortly after Laura's third birthday, my parents relieved us for a couple days so the two of us could take a short vacation alone. Before the end of our first day of respite, we received a phone call: Laura had suffered a brain seizure and was taken to the Intensive Care Unit. This hospital stay, her eighth in as many months, was short. Back home, we saw her ability to communicate slipping away. She would repeat the same sentences again and again. I had recently lost my grandmother who had become senile and repeated the same thing over and over. Observing such mental decline in a 93-year-old is one thing, but observing it in a three- year-old is another. Formerly a bright child and articulate speaker, Laura reached the point of endlessly mumbling the same pitiful question, "Does Amy love me?"

The anguish of watching her demise put my emotions through the wringer. Neither Beth nor I could talk about Laura publicly without becoming overwhelmed with sorrow and pain. Our congregation knew of our anguish, which surely must have defined our every expression, and we knew they prayed for us. We could not have made it through the ordeal without the support of our church. The folly of thinking that one can be a Christian and be isolated from the church was never more clear to me than during Laura's last months. Without asking for help or so much as hinting about our needs, we received an endless flow of grace and goodness. Meals appeared on the doorstep. An anonymous friend cut the lawn. A neighbor would take Amy for the afternoon so we could focus on Laura. Another friend would spend the night with both girls so we could get some sleep. This list goes on and on. As a cast set around a broken bone enables it to mend, so Christian love formed a cast around our breaking hearts and remained there later when our hearts were grieving.

Near the end of the summer, I requested an indefinite leave of absence from my pastoral duties. An examination of the spinal fluid around Laura's brain had revealed more cancer. The radiation, as the chemotherapy before it, had failed to destroy the tumor. It was now just a matter of time.

For the first time Beth and I dared to say aloud that Laura might not make it. Throughout the preceding months, we had tried to keep up hope for the sake of each other as for ourselves. Beth stopped lighting a candle every day as a symbol of hope. As Laura's death approached, an onslaught of grief set in. Beth wept openly and freely, as she had throughout the terrible ordeal. I envied her, for I had shed only a few tears. Tears were a new experience in my adult life, and I was afraid what might happen if I started to cry and could not stop. I was afraid because grief's tears can no more be controlled than the rain and yet, as the dry earth needs the rain, so my grieving soul needed to let the tears fall freely and fearlessly. Then one night it rained. My tears burst out as I realized I was losing my daughter, my little friend who had taught me so much about tenderness, innocence, patience and endurance. This cloudburst made me realize my inattention to my emotions. I had been so busy staying on top of Laura's medical procedures and her home care like a good manager would do that I had neglected matters of the heart — my own and Beth's.

Beth and I feel emotions, respond to problems and grieve differently. The loss of a child can be devastating to a marriage, even a good one like ours. Nearly 80 percent of marriages end in divorce after the death of a child, and I understand how this can happen. No two people deal with loss the same way. When grieving parents do not give each other the freedom to grieve in their own way, frustration and misunderstanding can lead to anger. "Why doesn't her death bother you more than it does?" "Why don't you get a grip on yourself and stop crying?" Grace can be found in accepting that each of us is unique and grieves in his or her own way.

Grieving parents often inadvertently blame each other or blame themselves. The words "if only" dominate thoughts and conversations. "If only you hadn't been so hesitant to push the doctors for an answer." "If only we had noticed her symptoms sooner." Grace can be found in replacing "if only" with "nevertheless." The Bible frequently uses this word when speaking of human frailty and fallibility. The Bible seldom, if ever, speaks in terms of "if only." Sure, we should have noticed Laura's walking problems sooner. Sure, we should have been more assertive early on in seeking a diagnosis. Maybe we should not have consented to the second major operation. Maybe we should not have pursued the radiation. Nevertheless, we are human and did the best we could.

Also, at this point came a recommendation to readmit Laura to the hospital. After a great deal of reflection and discussion, we decided to keep her at home in familiar surroundings with the people she knew and loved. Our living room became a hospital room, and our coffee table a pharmacy. We were on duty twenty-four hours a day administering drugs to control seizures and pain. Our lives became a nightmare of watching, waiting and wondering, "Will it be today or tonight?" Our prayers became pleas, "Lord, take her now. No more suffering. No more of this slow, senseless dying."

I admit now that on several occasions as I sat beside Laura's almost lifeless body, I thought about giving her a quicker, more peaceful exit from this life. At my disposal were an ample supply of morphine sulfate for her pain and Phenobarbital for her convulsions. A liberal administration of both would have put her to sleep once and for all. I now understand the emotional strain that leads to rash action on the part of a person who watches a loved one die a long, painful death. I understand how the word mercy is not out of place with the word killing. But I did not act on my impulses, for I believed then, as I do now, that life belongs to God. "The Lord gives and the Lord takes away." While I would do nothing to prolong Laura's life at this point, neither would I hasten her death. In retrospect, I would have admitted her to the hospital near the end. I think she would have received better pain management there, and the emotional toll of waiting and watching might have been less traumatic for Beth and me.

For more than two weeks our deathwatch persisted. Many nights I stayed awake beside a semi-conscious Laura, whose days and nights were reversed. During those quiet night watches, prayer became my ally. But the type of praying I did was different from what I had done before. Deep, heartfelt groans replaced the shallow cadence of words. I gained new insight into the Bible verse that reads, "The Spirit helps us in our weakness; for we do not know how to pray as we ought, but that very Spirit intercedes with sighs too deep for words" (Romans 8: 26 NRSV).

Later, my deep groans fell into a hushed and holy silence. I was reminded of Job's three friends who visited him after he had lost his possessions, his children and his health. They found their friend sitting in intense anguish. In one of the great acts of human kindness and wisdom, they simply sat with him in silence for seven days and nights. A Buddhist proverb says, "Do not speak unless you can improve on the silence." Those silent nights beside Laura and before God were holy nights during which I learned the value of simply sitting still before an awesome and mysterious Presence. Holy awe filled me, but so did holy anger! Why was all of this happening to such a wonderful little girl?

Laura took her last breath on the morning of August 29, 1986, one month after her third birthday. It was over. At the end, hers was a peaceful passing; mine was a restless remaining. While one common misconception is that the Bible holds a clear answer to our question of why, another misconception is that people of faith should not be angry with God or, if we are, we should never express that anger.

With no answer to why an innocent one suffers, anger is a natural outgrowth. How can we not feel angered frustration with this all-good, all-knowing, all-powerful God? Like grief, anger takes on different expressions in different people. This difference was a source of struggle between Beth and me. Her anger was more personal and emotional: "Why did this happen to my little girl?" My anger was more abstract and intellectual: "How could this happen to any little girl?" Expecting each other to deal with our shared loss in the same manner created tension between us. As we had to learn to let each other grieve in our own way, so we had to learn to let each deal with anger in our own way. One thing was certain: we had to give each other and ourselves the freedom to be angry at death, angry at life and angry with God. In the midst of deep personal loss, anger needs the First Amendment freedom of expression.

Sometimes We Stay Angry with God

Let me tell you how I tried to express my anger with God. For several months I had watched my little girl's life slowly waste away. First, she lost her ability to walk, then to sit, to swallow, to speak, to move anything but her eyes, then to see. All the while, I prayed she would lose her ability to breathe. During the last weeks of waiting for the end to come, my mind was overwhelmed with an image I could not shake. I pictured God sitting on the witness stand in a courtroom with me the hounding prosecutor who sought to unravel the twisted threads of a great injustice.

I was angry about what was happening to Laura. I was angry with God, and I wanted Him to know it. I wanted my day in court with God in the hot seat. I wanted the satisfaction of making God twist and squirm before my questioning, just as I had twisted and squirmed before my daughter's suffering. This image is not original: others have shared it, including God's own Son. In his moment of greatest anguish and confusion, Jesus cried out from the cross, "My God, My God, why have you forsaken me?" (Matthew 27: 46 NRSV). However, it is Job who most fully incarnates my image of God on the witness stand, for it is Job who pleads, "But I would speak to the Almighty, and I desire to argue my case with God." (Job 13: 3 NRSV). Reflecting upon the story of Job, I took the role of an aggressive prosecutor as I prepared my case against God. I believed then, and still do now, that I have a strong case against the injustice done to my little girl and to me. What follows is the imaginary transcript of that courtroom scene:

Prosecutor: I call to the stand the defendant in this case, God, who is accused of a gross and cruel injustice. Please reveal your identity to the court.

God: I am the Almighty Creator, Sustainer and Redeemer.

Prosecutor: Almighty God, for what reason did you create us?

God: I created you for one very simple reason; love. I created you out of my love.

Prosecutor: So it was your love for us that brought us into being. Does your love move beyond your act of creation? Do you continue to sustain us and to care for us out of love?

God: Yes.

Prosecutor: Well, then, perhaps you can explain to the court why you did not sustain and care for my daughter. Are the deists right? After you create, do you step into retirement, no longer taking an active role in our world and our lives?

God: Many believe that. However, I do not believe you do. Think back over your life, Mr. Prosecutor. Recall the opportunities, the disappointments and the milestones. On those occasions you acknowledged my presence and involvement. Can you now honestly deny my hand in your life?

Prosecutor: Well, then, maybe your activity is not so benevolent as we think it is. Maybe the fruit of your hand is bitter instead of sweet. Maybe your works are

28

no different from ours, that is, a mixture of good and evil.

God: Before I respond, we need to define what is meant by "good" and "evil." Most people, I have observed, define as good only those things that they enjoy and bring them immediate benefit. Therefore, their definition of evil is anything that blocks the attainment of good, or joy and enjoyment. Both good and evil become totally subjective and defined solely on the basis of self.

Prosecutor: How can life be otherwise? How else can one define good and evil apart from personal experience?

God: Mr. Prosecutor, you must begin to peel away this thin veneer you call faith, a faith that looks to me only for personal pleasure and gain. You must begin to reach for meaning that transcends the moment and present circumstances. Good and evil have meanings far greater than your pleasure and your sorrow. In the midst of personal tragedy, many have called me a cruel God. They do so when they view the events of life solely from the viewpoint of the moment. They want clear, crisp answers for every dilemma right now. Faith will not grant such a wish. Faith gives one an eternal perspective that is not offended by the mystery of the moment.

Prosecutor: God, you used the word "mystery." Perhaps you are no more than my own creation to fill the intellectual gaps and provide an explanation for life's mysteries. Let me ask it more directly. God, do you really exist as the all-powerful sovereign of the universe, or are you merely the attempt of my mind and heart to explain the unexplainable?

God: Again, my answer comes by way of asking you to reflect upon the awesomeness of life and the intimate events of your life. Do you believe that I am your creator? Do you find comfort in thinking that you are master of your own destiny, and humankind is master of the world's destiny? Or will you believe that you are the creation of my purposes? The choice is yours.

Prosecutor: I want to get to the pressing question at hand. Earlier you identified yourself as the Sustainer and caring Protector of your creation. Why did you withdraw your care from my family? Why have we lost favor in your eyes?

God: On what grounds do you make such accusations? Do you know me only through your circumstances? Do you call me a caring Sustainer only when health and happiness prevail? Do I cease to be good and loving the moment hardship strikes? Cannot my purposes and promises exceed your understanding?

Prosecutor: I agree with your logic. But why, in your greatness, did you not intervene to change my circumstances? Why did you not reverse the progression of Laura's cancer? Certainly such action is within your power.

God: Humankind demands freedom in life. In my love, I have made you more than puppets in a predetermined play. Yet when life run its course, you cry foul and complain about where the path leads you. You want two things that cannot exist together - life's absolute freedom and my absolute control.

Prosecutor: But which is it?

God: I created life to be a strange and wonderful mixture of freedom and control, randomness and providence, chaos and order, chance and purpose. In my love for your life and for all of life, I have woven together a tapestry in which strength can arise from weakness, light from darkness, meaning from mystery, and life from death. Life is not an intellectual riddle to be solved; it is a mysterious gift to be embraced.

Prosecutor: God, if you are the loving Creator and Sustainer as you claim, why have you taken from me that which is mine, my little girl, the source of my joy? An injustice began the moment you began to take what belonged to me!

God: Mr. Prosecutor, you speak as if you possessed the rights over creation. Let me ask you something: were you there when I brought the world into existence? Were you the one, and not I, who gave Laura life? You complain about losing something that never belonged to you in the first place. Laura was a gift to you for a time. Never forget she is mine for all time.

Prosecutor: God, I speak now from my heart rather than solely from my mind. When I put away my intellectual arguments, my heart cries out, "You don't know what it is like to watch your child slowly die! You have no idea how I hurt!"

God: You forget that I do know what it is like to lose a child, my only Son.

Prosecutor: That is my point. Your Son suffered and died, but what is death to one who had the resurrection awaiting him? It is different for you!

God: Do you not think his suffering was real? His death was terrifying to him and agonizing for me!

Prosecutor: I do not deny the reality of his death. However, he had the resurrection awaiting him. He had hope within his grasp.

God: Is not the same hope available to you? You need more than a creator and sustainer who guards life as it exists at this moment. You need a redeemer, who can ensure life and love beyond the moment; one who can heal the nagging "if onlys" and calm the angry "whys," and who can fulfill life's unfilled dreams. I can restore that which is broken, save that which is lost, and resurrect that which is dead. I give life, and I give new life.

Prosecutor: I believe that, but I still do not understand why my little girl had to be the subject of your theory. It does not make sense that this should be tested on a three-year-old. I cannot understand such happenings.

God: Nor will you fully understand. You said you are speaking from the heart and not solely from the mind. This is the stage I have wanted you to reach. Your mind tries to control life by demanding explanations and answers. The heart has greater need.

Prosecutor: But how can I give you my heart when my head spins with unanswered questions and unrelieved anger?

God: You cannot do this on your own. That is why I have given you my Holy Spirit to live inside your heart and enable it to embrace the mysteries that your mind cannot fathom. You need meaning in tragedy more than you need to understand tragedy. You need love to fill the void. You need hope in a painfully depriving world. You ask my reasons. They are beyond you. But I am within your grasp. I am the center of all life. I can bring meaning to the most perplexing mysteries. I ask only that you trust me. No matter how confusing and painful the moment might be, you must trust me. You do not need my answers; you need my presence.

Prosecutor: How can I trust when I have lost something more precious to me than my own life? How can I trust in the face of irreplaceable loss? But yet, how can I not trust when I see how fragile life is? How can I not trust when I recall that there is always a mysterious gap of understanding between life's Giver and life's recipients, between the Potter and the clay? I'm trying to trust you, O Lord, but it is not easy. The trust I do have does not ease my pain or calm my anger. Nevertheless, I know that I need your presence in my life even more than I long for Laura's presence in my life. I need your presence in my suffering more than I need an explanation for my suffering. But O God, it so hard, so very, very hard, to keep going.

. . . . .

This is how I felt. You might think that putting God in the position of having to answer to me, a mere mortal, was too bold. But if you were honest with yourself, you would admit to wanting to do the same thing in the face of your anger. Or you might feel that I was too easy on God by letting Him out of the hot seat too soon. I will admit that I have angrily recalled the Lord to the witness stand on several occasions since then. As you deal with your anger, you may want to seek an extension in order not to let God's trial end too soon. The Lord, in His great love and patience, will stay on the witness stand as long as you need Him there. God's love for us is big enough to handle our anger, if we will only let it out. Anger is essential to the grieving process, and grief is essential to faith's ability to survive a loss.

Moving Through Our Grieving

We live in a world where everything has a title or label. We even have special titles for those who grieve. A woman who loses a husband is a widow. A husband who loses a wife is a widower. A child who loses parents is an orphan. But what do we call a parent who loses a child? "Bereaved" is too theoretical, too polite. It does not capture the nausea that fills my gut when I think of my daughter's death and the loss of what could have been. Calling me an "inspiration" does not work either. It is too patronizing. I do not want to be an inspiration of strength and courage to others in my loss. I want to be my little girl's daddy and to have her grow up before my eyes. While no title can adequately express my pain at Laura's death, one thing is sure: I am still grieving.

The process of grieving confronts us with some of the hardest choices we must make in life. Will we shake our fist and curse God, or will we open our hand and seek God? On September 3, 1986, I stood before an open grave over which a small white coffin hung suspended between heaven and earth. I believe that in life and in death we belong to God and that God's mercy is never ending. However, the mercy of this God is so severe at times.

Words cannot express my feelings as I think about my daughter. I watched her take her first breath and her last. At her birth, I watched as she was placed into the warm arms of her mother and at her burial, as she was lowered into the cold arms of her grave. As a pastor, I have become adept at enduring others' heartaches. I am able to speak to them about being open to God's purposes despite the pain. However, when it is my own heartache and my own quest for a purpose amidst the pain, it is entirely another matter.

When I speak of divine purpose, I do not believe for one moment that God sent or caused Laura's tumor. God is not cruel. As I try to grasp what place God has in my life's events, I recognize that He can use my tragedy to teach me something. So what has God taught me through Laura's ordeal and death? To tell you the truth, class is still in session, and I suspect it will be for some time.

However, I share with you two insights I have learned so far, or which have at least been reinforced in me. First, God speaks to us in the hardest of times. If we listen, God can be heard amid the cries that pour out of broken hearts. Second, in everything that happens in life there is an opportunity to strengthen faith and enrich an appreciation for life. The real tragedy in a tragedy occurs when those involved do not allow the event to deepen their love for the Giver and the gift of life.

Grieving confronts us with another tough choice. Will we run from our pain or move through it? My advice is try to stay connected with your faith and with other people. Fight the urge to run away, since isolation derails the grieving process and delays the healing. Like an athlete who must play through pain, so a grieving parent must face the pain in order to move through it. At Laura's funeral, a good friend who conducted the service reminded all of the need to remain connected with God. When the pain is deep, we can echo Jesus' cry from the cross, "My God, My God, why have you forsaken me?" As we cry those words, remember, "My God, My God." This God, who is my God and your God, does not abandon us in times of tragedy and grief. I am convinced that the tears Beth and I shed over Laura's death were surpassed only by the tears God shed for her. God remains connected to us and to our pain. Stay connected with your faith.

Get yourself back to church, painful though it may be. Sit near the back so that when a hymn or thought triggers uncontrollable tears, you can step outside. Even now I have a hard time getting through the hymn, "Be Still, My Soul," which we sang at Laura's funeral. My heart sticks in my throat when I sing that last verse:

> Be still, my soul! The hour is hast'ning on
> When we shall be forever with the Lord,
> When disappointment, grief and fear are gone,
> Sorrow forgot, love's purest joys restored.
> Be still, my soul! When change and tears are past;
> All safe and blessed we shall meet at last.

My tears are not yet past. And they still need to flow in the presence of those who share my faith and hope.

Grief reduces us to zombies, as we surrealistically move through space and go through the motions slowly. We attend church, but we feel no joy. That's okay. Just going through the motions may be all we can do at the time. At least we are moving forward. On many Sundays after Laura's death, as I stood before the congregation leading worship, I felt I was just going through the motions. But at least I was in motion.

Conducting funerals was particularly hard for me right after Laura's death. So was preaching. I would often look out into the congregation and see someone who had helped shoulder our suffering. Those faces evoked a flood of emotion within me. To prevent my anguish from spilling out at the wrong time — like in the middle of a sermon — I had to give myself time to grieve openly at home. The tears that were once rare flowed often in the weeks after Laura's death. For several months I set aside time every week to sit alone and look through photos of Laura in order to elicit my tears. These controlled releases of emotion at home helped avoid uncontrolled riots of emotion in public. Eventually, I abandoned this practice, convinced I was beyond the need to prompt my tears. Then one Sunday as I was preaching on a topic that was, as I recall, not connected to my loss, I suddenly became overwhelmed with grief. My throat tightened, my voice cracked and my tears flowed. Frustrated and exasperated by my inability to control my emotions, I inadvertently let fly an expletive as I said aloud, "@#$%, I didn't want this to happen anymore!" My congregation graciously understood my frustration, and I learned about the undeniable power of grief. If we do not let it out regularly, it will come roaring out on its own.

The experience of connecting with other parents who have lost a child to cancer was a great help in the grieving process. They reminded me that I was not alone in my feelings of loss, pain and confusion. Beth found this support group less helpful and sought out personal counseling as a means of addressing her grief. Find some context where you can talk about your pain with others who will listen and let you talk.

Friends also proved to be an invaluable gift of grace. Now, as then, the greatest gift any friend can give to Beth and me is to invite us to recall something about Laura. When friends who knew Laura say, "I remember when Laura did this…. or said that…," and when friends who did not know her say, "Tell me one of your fondest memories," it is an invitation to celebrate her life. Granted, emotion swells and tears flow, but the opportunity to talk with others about our little girl is another expression of mercy.

A few weeks after Laura's death, a friend of ours visited Beth. Wanting to broach the subject of Laura's death but not sure what to say, she asked, "So, do you still miss Laura?" (This would have been a good time for our friend to follow the lead of Job's friends who sat with him in silence.) Dumbfounded by the question, Beth replied, "I will always miss Laura." When a child dies, a part of the parents dies, too. Recovery is an ongoing process. We will never get over our loss. We will never stop missing Laura.

At a clergy meeting several months after Laura's death, a colleague asked how I was doing. He was genuinely interested in my answer. He allowed me to do the talking and patiently listened. Another pastor I did not know overheard our conversation and interrupted. He then proceeded to tell me about his own child who had been sick and hospitalized before launching into a sermon about believing in God in the hard times. One pastor used my loss to invite me to talk as he listened. The other used my loss as an occasion for him to "preach" at me. Which one do you think proved more helpful? Go and do likewise!

I do not give much weight to the concept of bringing closure to grief. Grief is not something we complete like a homework assignment. A third misunderstanding I have discovered is that Christians feel they should move beyond their time of grief. This assumes that grief can be confined to a definite time slot in our life. Grief is not so manageable, because grief is not an event. For this reason, I choose to speak of my grieving, rather than my grief. The idea of bringing closure to my grieving for Laura suggests to me closing a door on her life and on my life with her. I realize that I must reconcile to my loss of her and accept the absence of her presence as well as the presence of her absence. However, I never want to close the door completely on my pain. To end my grieving for her would seem, somehow, to end my loving of her. With time, my grieving changes. It must. However, to the thought of my grieving ending completely, I say, it must not!

When we are moving through our own grieving or helping others move through theirs, the following words written by Frederick Buechner remind us that the process needs to move forward.

> Even the saddest things can become, once we have made peace with them, a source of wisdom and strength for the journey that still lies ahead.[1]

Looking Toward What's Next

In the weeks immediately following Laura's funeral, I visited her grave every day. Whether I was driving somewhere or taking an early morning run, I managed to direct my travels past the cemetery. There at her gravesite, I paused for brief sojourns into my memory. The first few visits were as serene and beautiful as the funeral bouquets were vibrant in their color and form. Their vitality gave birth to memories of Laura's exuberant life before her illness. But as the flowers withered, so did my thoughts. Staring at a mound of browning petals, I became transfixed with the graying power of death. My thoughts of Laura's lively past became overshadowed by my dismay over her absence. This led to questions about her future.

The hope of eternal life was anchored firmly in my convictions, but my questions about what it will be like became more pressing than ever. Standing over Laura's entombed body, I pondered the hows, wheres and whens of what's next. Especially, what's next for Laura.

Some respond with, "Nothing. This is it!" Yes, some people hold that there is nothing meaningful or permanent in this existence of ours and nothing beyond this life. If nothing comes next, what a cruel hoax it is to be born in the first place! Thank God other options are available.

A different reply dominated Old Testament thinking: We will be confined to the gray, listless realm of the dead called Sheol. This is a bleak view of life after death. Life after death in much of the Old Testament was understood in terms of living on through one's descendants. The community kept alive the deceased in their memories, but the individual remained in the place of the dead.

Reincarnation into other life forms is the afterlife viewed in the Hindu religion. They say we go around again and again until we get our lives straightened out and achieve oneness with God. This belief arises from the conviction that human history is an endless cycle. Such a view is not harmonious with the Judeo-Christian belief that history has a definite beginning and end, and that each life has a single start and finish on this earth.

A fourth consideration of life after death emerges from ancient Greek philosophy, with its conviction about the immortality of the soul. They believed our soul survives death and enters a state of bliss. The body is lost forever. According to the Greeks, this should be of no concern, since the body is inferior to the soul and it is the soul alone that counts. Contemporary writers on the subject of death who have adopted this view embrace the immortality of the soul (the indestructibility of the personality), but say nothing about the resurrection of the body. This perspective fails to address the whole person as God created us, body and soul.

The Christian hope is built not upon the immortality of the soul, but upon the resurrection of the dead. Our hope of life after death stands not upon the soul's inherent ability to be immortal, but on God's gracious act of resurrecting the dead. What's next? The Christian response is best expressed in the concluding declarations of the Apostles' Creed, "I believe in the communion of the saints… the resurrection of the body and the life everlasting." When I say the Creed, I find myself fighting back tears. My little girl's death has given me new certainty and conviction in those final articles of faith. Through Jesus' resurrection, we carry the assurance of our own resurrection. Individuality does survive beyond the grave. You and I continue to be ourselves, not just immortal souls floating through eternity, but total persons with body and soul united in everlasting life with all those who have preceded us into the full presence of God.

Yet our faith offers few details, if any, about the nature of eternal life. When we speak of it, we are speaking of a life that transcends our language, experience, and concepts of time and space. The difficulty in describing heaven is that we have no past or present life events to which it can be compared. Thus, talk of eternal life to those on this side of the grave is like describing a colorful sunset to a person who was born blind. Despite our inability to grasp the heavenly vision, those of us whose loved one has taken up residence in the afterlife yearn for a clearer picture of it. As I think about Laura's absence from this life and presence in the one beyond, the question of what's next has given birth to other questions.

I wonder what heaven is like. Eternal life was a vague and unexamined concept until I began to think of Laura's presence there. The place we live takes on the character of who we are and how we live. Our homes reflect ourselves. Should it not be the same with our eternal home? I believe I now know a little more about heaven, for I know much about one of its residents.

I wonder about the person whose body is ravaged by disease. Will the emaciated torso be resurrected? My last visual memory of Laura was a gaunt corpse devastated by cancer. Into what will she be resurrected? If God could create the world out of nothing, cannot God do the same in resurrection? The Lord does not need embalmed bodies in cemeteries to fulfill His eternal purpose. Out of a diseased and dying world, He makes all things new. Crippled bodies will be made right. Handicapped minds will exceed their earthly limitations. Broken relationships will be reconciled. All things will be made new and complete.

I wonder if people will be eternally fixed at the age they died. If not, how will we recognize them? How will I recognize Laura when my time comes to see her again? Whatever else heaven may be, it is surely perfection and completeness. We imperfect humans will reach our full potential as image bearers of God. Age will become superfluous, as I would imagine appearances and achievements will in such a realm of fulfillment. Perhaps we will possess any age or all ages in heaven. Like bumping into an acquaintance you have not seen in years, there will be something recognizable about the person that transcends age or appearance.

I wonder if those who enter eternal life are lonely for those they leave behind. This question was very pressing for both Beth and me, as we thought of Laura entering a realm where she does not know anyone. Does she miss us? Certainly not as much as we miss her. Is she lonely? During one of the many setbacks before her death, I began to accept the likelihood that she would not survive. At that time, I had a dream, or a vision or thought, where Laura had died and was moving into eternal life. I envisioned my grandmother, a woman of great faith who had died a couple of years earlier, standing there, awaiting Laura with open arms. Although Laura knew no one in God's heaven, she was known. As is the case with God's embracing love, we are known before we know and loved before we love.

What's next for mine and yours? We can suggest, but

cannot know. Whatever is next for them will be better than what is now. There will be more joy, more love and more life than ever before. To borrow a thought from William Wordsworth:

> We shall see again those things and those ones
> we now see no more; and the glory that passed
> away from earth shall return to us in even greater glory.[2]

So what about us? Having considered what's next for those whom we have loved and lost, we wonder what's next for those who remain here grieving. How I miss Laura Grace, my beautiful gift, who was an education in tenderness and love! How much I miss the times we played and talked and laughed together. Those times were the very essence of what life is meant to be. When we are in the long process of grieving, we need to recapture that essence of life, especially the ability to laugh again. A grieving parent's ability to regain laughter is as essential as a drowning person's ability to regain breath. I offer no advice on how to do this, I merely declare its importance. I will never forget how that lesson was brought home to me. Shortly after Laura's death, I received a letter written by a young woman whose first child died shortly after birth and whose second child had the same type of brain cancer Laura had. This grieving mother, before whose pain I felt like a rookie, shared with me the daily prayer she offers which helps her faith survive her loss, "Lord, teach us to laugh again, but never let us forget that we have cried."

Although I have regained my ability to laugh, pain and sorrow frequently return with the same intensity I felt the first time I heard the diagnosis of cancer, and the moment I saw Laura take her last breath. Will my storm of tears ever begin to subside? Will I ever find the light that dissolves the dismal shadows of anguish? I want no hasty escape from the pain, for it reveals the depth of my love for Laura. What I need and desire is the strength to move ahead with life, despite the recurring torrents of emotion. Such strength can only be found in the hope that God breathes into an exhausted heart.

Throughout Laura's illness, thousands of people around the country prayed for her healing. Since her death, I am often asked why these prayers were not answered. An unknown source offers these words of perspective: "Nothing lies outside the reach of prayer except that which lies outside the will of God." This insight raises a new question as to why Laura's healing was not within the will of God. Emily Dickinson wondered, too, and said:

> I shall know why - when Time is over
> And I have ceased to wonder why.
> Christ will explain each separate anguish
> In the fair schoolroom of the sky.[3]

We will always have unanswered questions with respect to the tragedies of this life. I know I still do.

Sources

[1] Frederick Buechner, *Telling Secrets* (San Francisco: Harper San Francisco, 1991), pg 33.

[2] William Wordsworth, "Ode: Intimations of Immortality from Recollections of Early Childhood," contained in Frederick Nims, *The Harper Anthology of Poetry* (New York: Harper and Row, 1981), pg 257.

[3] Emily Dickinson, "I Shall Know Why," No. 193 contained in Thomas H. Johnson, ed., *The Poems of Emily Dickinson* (Boston: Little, Brown and Co., 1955), pg 91.

Suggestions for Further Reading

Frankl, Viktor E. *Man's Search for Meaning.* New York: Simon & Schuster, 1959.
>A Jewish psychiatrist and Nazi death camp survivor tells of the need to find meaning in the face of pain and despair in order to survive.

Hans, Daniel T. *God on the Witness Stand.* Grand Rapids: Baker Book House, 1989. (Out of Print)
>A collection of eight sermons that I preached during my daughter's illness and immediately following her death. Photocopies may be obtained by contacting: Gettysburg Presbyterian Church, 208 Baltimore St. Gettysburg, PA 17325.

Lewis, C. S. *A Grief Observed.* New York: Seabury Press, 1961.
>This great Christian writer reflects upon the premature death of his wife after their short time together.

Lewis, C. S. *The Problem of Pain.* New York: Macmillan & Co., 1962.
>Lewis presents a powerful Christian argument for faith in God in the face of the perplexing dilemma of pain and suffering.

Nouwen, Henri J. *A Letter of Consolation.* San Francisco: Harper & Row, 1982.

> This deeply spiritual priest and gifted writer composes a letter of consolation to his father and himself shortly after his mother's death.

Sittser, Gerald A. *A Grace Disguised: How the Soul Grows through Loss.* Grand Rapids: Zondervan, 1996.

> If you read only one book on grief and loss, make it this one! A grieving father tells of the survival of his two children and his faith and hope after the deaths of his mother, wife and young daughter in the same accident.

Vanauken, Sheldon. *A Severe Mercy.* San Francisco: Harper & Row, 1977.

> A young widower corresponds with C. S. Lewis about the fatal illness of his young wife.

Westberg, Granger E. *Good Grief.* Philadelphia: Fortress Press, 1962.

> One of the most popular books during the past three decades on handling the loss of a loved one. I give this to my grieving church members.

Wolterstorff, Nicholas. *Lament for a Son.* Grand Rapids: Eerdmans, 1987.

> A seminary professor and father reflects theologically and personally upon the sudden death of his young adult son.

Yancey, Philip. *Where Is God When It Hurts?* Grand Rapids: Zondervan, 1977.

>The title of this terrifically honest, award-winning book says it all.

Internet. *Crisis, Grief and Healing Page.*
http://www.webhealing.com/honor.html.

>Tom Golden, LCSW, offers this web site as a place where grieving parents can write tributes to and share reflections about their deceased children. The site also offers opportunity to e-mail other grieving parents.

OTHER
DESERT MINISTRIES, INC.
PUBLICATIONS

How To Live With Cancer

Como Vivir Con Cancer

Christ Will See You Through

When You Lose Someone You Love

The Future Is Now

The Rhapsody of Scripture

When Alzheimer's Disease Strikes

Prayers Against Depression

God's Promises & My Needs

How To Help An Alcoholic

You Now Have Custody Of You

My Adventures With Mankind

Humor and Healing

Reflections On Suicide

Write to:
Desert Ministries, Inc.
P.O. Box 788
Palm Beach, FL 33480
Or
Fax (561) 832-0279